The Choice

Creator and illustrator: Patrick Arguin

English translation: Bleu Dactylo

French version written by: Michèle Rappe
Support, coaching and collaboration: Hélène Beaudette

I want to offer my deepest gratitude to Hélène Beaudette.
Her unconditional support and presence allowed TOOLS OF THE HEART to grow and come into form.

Colin and Fluffy are now good friends.
This morning, the little squirrel is enjoying breakfast in the company of his friend the oak. How sweet it is to share these moments together!

Suddenly, a raccoon approaches.
It seems to be looking for something in
Colin's branches.

«Hello there oak,» says the raccoon.
«I am Grubber, how about you?»
«My name is Colin, and this is my friend Fluffy.»

But the raccoon barely listens to Colin's response and does not even look at Fluffy. Colin's heart begins to cringe a little.

«I want acorns!» says Grubber.
Colin thinks that the raccoon is very impolite and does not like it.

However, he still allows him to climb up and pick some acorns.

«You can take three,» says Colin, «the others are for my friend Fluffy.»
«All right! Just three!» says Grubber.

Grubber climbs up and helps himself, but gobbles up 10 acorns! «Hey! I told you to take only three!» cries Colin in a sad voice. «Bah! It does not matter!» replies Grubber, fleeing the scene.

Colin is very upset. He wanted to be nice to the raccoon, but Grubber chose to lie and steal acorns. Colin feels betrayed.

«I will never give acorns to anyone again!» he says. «All raccoons are not like Grubber,» answers Fluffy.

Fluffy does not know what to say to comfort his friend but stays with him and listens to his friend's sadness.

Colin remembers that whenever he feels sad, he can go into his heart to feel well again. He then takes three deep and long breaths and thinks about his rainbow of wisdom.

Colin feels more and more calm. Blue, the elf, appears before him. «Think about the moment you met Grubber,» says the elf, «and remember how it started.»

Colin remembers Grubber being rude, barely saying hello and demanding acorns.

Blue continues, «do you feel Grubber was respectful with you? Do you think it was polite of him to act that way with you?»

«No,» says Colin, «it was not very kind of him, it was also very unpleasant!»

«My dear Colin, your heart has felt Grubber's attitude, but you chose to let him climb up your branches anyway. You have learned an important lesson here.»

«When you feel that people are impolite, you have the right to say you don't appreciate it. And you could have chosen not to give away your acorns. It is important to listen to your heart.»

Colin thanks Blue and opens up his eyes.
Suddenly, he sees a raccoon approaching!

Nervous, Fluffy climbs up to the highest branch
to get a better look. Colin starts to feel nervous too.

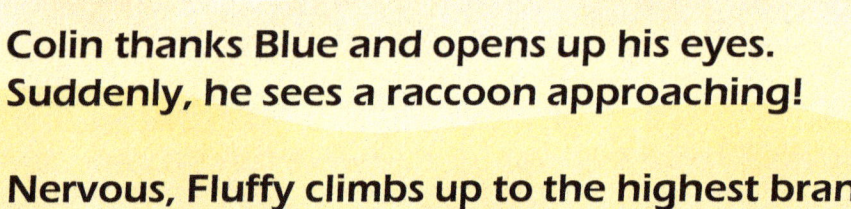

«Hello, you two!» cheerfully says the raccoon.
«Hello!» answer the two friends.

«My name is Hazel. We have never met before.
I live on the other side of the river.
I am hungry, and my house is far away!»

«Would you be willing to share one or two acorns please?»

Colin focuses on his feelings. The attitude of this raccoon is different than Grubber's. More importantly, in his heart everything is calm. Colin chooses to give Hazel some acorns.

«Thank you very much,» says the raccoon, «have a nice day!»
«You were right Fluffy; all raccoons are not alike!»

What a day!
Colin and Fluffy are peacefully enjoying Father Sun's last rays. Soon, the day's commotion will quiet, and the Moon will watch over the beloved garden.

Remember...

How can I know if I can trust someone?

Be mindful of what you are feeling. If you hesitate, or if you feel uneasy with someone, take the time to verify what it is you are sensing in your heart. If you need to, talk to an adult.

Is it important to always tell the truth?

A lie is like a rock that you carry with you all the time. It can become heavy and uncomfortable. Telling the truth may feel scary sometimes, but lying is never a good solution.

What can I do when telling the truth feels difficult?

Look inside your heart to know why it is difficult. Maybe you fear the other person's reaction, or you fear getting punished. You can admit to the person that you are scared, before saying you still choose to share the truth with him or her.

The Book Collection

Tools of the Heart
Fostering Confidence and Self-esteem

1 Father Sun and Mother Earth Create Life
Breathing/Finding your rhythm

Breathing is essential to life; conscious breathing is a simple, yet effective way to regain your calm and well-being by finding your body's rhythm.

2 Fluffy and the Rainbow in his Heart
Meditation/Finding your inner calm

Each one of us has a peaceful place inside their heart. Meditation is a tool that allows you to find your personal space or to go back to it.

3 Colin Discovers Confidence
Grounding/Strengthening your self-confidence

Growing up often comes with its share of fears and hesitations. Growing solid roots helps to build and nurture a positive self-confidence.

4 Colin and Fluffy Become Friends
Knowing yourself/Loving and appreciating

Positive self-confidence and self-esteem are the building blocks of healthy relationships; therefore, learning to appreciate who we are is a treasure for life.

5 The Choice
Insight/Listening to your intuition

Learning to listen to your inner voice and how to trust it, is learning to stay true to yourself in all situations.

6 Colin's Courage
Expressing/Confidence in yourself

Standing up for yourself is not wrong. It is about relying on your self-worth with confidence, to respectfully say what you need to say.

7 Enough is Enough
Self-respect/Daring to be yourself

Developing good communication skills also implies expressing your feelings and needs in a respectful manner, which can sometimes be a challenge!

8 Fluffy Finds his Well-being
Self-awareness/Taking responsibility

Growing up is also about becoming more aware of your emotions and learning to manage them responsibly.

The Meditation Collection

Tools of the Heart
Fostering Confidence and Self-esteem

Specially designed for young children, the guided meditations explore and develop the same themes, as seen in the **Tools of the Heart** book collection. These intend to reinforce the children's knowledge of themselves through their inner space of wisdom, where things can be seen, heard, and felt.

Meditation is also a wonderful tool that children can easily learn to help them self-regulate physically, mentally, and emotionally.

To learn more, go to our website:
www.toolsoftheheart.com

www.ingramcontent.com/pod-product-compliance
Lightning Source LLC
Chambersburg PA
CBHW041159120626

46547CB00020B/3264